Online Course Tracker

Helps you keep track of your online course purchases and be able to easily log back in to your courses even if it has been weeks, months, or years since your last log in.

Table of Contents

Table of Contents

Table of Contents

Course Name	Page Number

Table of Contents

"An investment in knowledge pays the best interest."

- Abraham Lincoln

Course title: _____

Instructor name: _____

Date of purchase: _____ Amount Paid: _____

Email address used for purchase: _____

Date email confirmation was received: _____

Email confirmation sent from: _____

Order # from email confirmation: _____

Does course come with a satisfaction guarantee?   Yes / No   If yes,

when does guarantee expire? _____

Lifetime access to course material? Yes / No   If no, when does access

expire? _____

Log in URL: _____

User name: _____ Password: _____

Is any bonus content included with purchase?   Yes / No

If yes, list bonus content and when it is to be released here:

_____

_____

_____

_____

_____

_____

_____

_____

Lessons / Modules that I have found to be particularly helpful or interesting:

_____

_____

_____

_____

_____

Course title: _____

Instructor name: _____

Date of purchase: _____ Amount Paid: _____

Email address used for purchase: _____

Date email confirmation was received: _____

Email confirmation sent from: _____

Order # from email confirmation: _____

Does course come with a satisfaction guarantee?   Yes / No   If yes,

when does guarantee expire? _____

Lifetime access to course material? Yes / No   If no, when does access

expire? _____

Log in URL: _____

User name: _____ Password: _____

Is any bonus content included with purchase?   Yes / No

If yes, list bonus content and when it is to be released here:

_____

_____

_____

_____

_____

_____

_____

_____

Lessons / Modules that I have found to be particularly helpful or interesting:

_____

_____

_____

_____

_____

Course title: _____

Instructor name: _____

Date of purchase: _____ Amount Paid: _____

Email address used for purchase: _____

Date email confirmation was received: _____

Email confirmation sent from: _____

Order # from email confirmation: _____

Does course come with a satisfaction guarantee?   Yes / No   If yes,

when does guarantee expire? _____

Lifetime access to course material? Yes / No   If no, when does access

expire? _____

Log in URL: _____

User name: _____ Password: _____

Is any bonus content included with purchase?   Yes / No

If yes, list bonus content and when it is to be released here:

_____

_____

_____

_____

_____

_____

_____

_____

Lessons / Modules that I have found to be particularly helpful or interesting:

_____

_____

_____

_____

_____

Course title: _____

Instructor name: _____

Date of purchase: _____ Amount Paid: _____

Email address used for purchase: _____

Date email confirmation was received: _____

Email confirmation sent from: _____

Order # from email confirmation: _____

Does course come with a satisfaction guarantee?   Yes / No   If yes, when does guarantee expire? _____

Lifetime access to course material?   Yes / No   If no, when does access expire? _____

Log in URL: _____

User name: _____ Password: _____

Is any bonus content included with purchase?   Yes / No

If yes, list bonus content and when it is to be released here:

_____

_____

_____

_____

_____

_____

_____

_____

Lessons / Modules that I have found to be particularly helpful or interesting:

_____

_____

_____

_____

_____

Course title: _____

Instructor name: _____

Date of purchase: _____ Amount Paid: _____

Email address used for purchase: _____

Date email confirmation was received: _____

Email confirmation sent from: _____

Order # from email confirmation: _____

Does course come with a satisfaction guarantee?   Yes / No   If yes, when does guarantee expire? _____

Lifetime access to course material? Yes / No   If no, when does access expire? _____

Log in URL: _____

User name: _____ Password: _____

Is any bonus content included with purchase?   Yes / No

If yes, list bonus content and when it is to be released here:

_____

_____

_____

_____

_____

_____

_____

_____

Lessons / Modules that I have found to be particularly helpful or interesting:

_____

_____

_____

_____

_____

Course title: _____

Instructor name: _____

Date of purchase: _____ Amount Paid: _____

Email address used for purchase: _____

Date email confirmation was received: _____

Email confirmation sent from: _____

Order # from email confirmation: _____

Does course come with a satisfaction guarantee?   Yes / No   If yes,

when does guarantee expire? _____

Lifetime access to course material?   Yes / No   If no, when does access

expire? _____

Log in URL: _____

User name: _____ Password: _____

Is any bonus content included with purchase?   Yes / No

If yes, list bonus content and when it is to be released here:

_____

_____

_____

_____

_____

_____

_____

_____

_____

Lessons / Modules that I have found to be particularly helpful or interesting:

_____

_____

_____

_____

_____

Course title: _____

Instructor name: _____

Date of purchase: _____ Amount Paid: _____

Email address used for purchase: _____

Date email confirmation was received: _____

Email confirmation sent from: _____

Order # from email confirmation: _____

Does course come with a satisfaction guarantee?   Yes / No   If yes,

when does guarantee expire? _____

Lifetime access to course material? Yes / No   If no, when does access

expire? _____

Log in URL: _____

User name: _____ Password: _____

Is any bonus content included with purchase?   Yes / No

If yes, list bonus content and when it is to be released here:

_____

_____

_____

_____

_____

_____

_____

_____

Lessons / Modules that I have found to be particularly helpful or interesting:

_____

_____

_____

_____

_____

Course title: _____

Instructor name: _____

Date of purchase: _____ Amount Paid: _____

Email address used for purchase: _____

Date email confirmation was received: _____

Email confirmation sent from: _____

Order # from email confirmation: _____

Does course come with a satisfaction guarantee?   Yes / No   If yes,

when does guarantee expire? _____

Lifetime access to course material?   Yes / No   If no, when does access

expire? _____

Log in URL: _____

User name: _____ Password: _____

Is any bonus content included with purchase?   Yes / No

If yes, list bonus content and when it is to be released here:

_____

_____

_____

_____

_____

_____

_____

_____

Lessons / Modules that I have found to be particularly helpful or interesting:

_____

_____

_____

_____

_____

Course title: _____

Instructor name: _____

Date of purchase: _____ Amount Paid: _____

Email address used for purchase: _____

Date email confirmation was received: _____

Email confirmation sent from: _____

Order # from email confirmation: _____

Does course come with a satisfaction guarantee?   Yes / No   If yes,

when does guarantee expire? _____

Lifetime access to course material? Yes / No   If no, when does access

expire? _____

Log in URL: _____

User name: _____ Password: _____

Is any bonus content included with purchase?   Yes / No

If yes, list bonus content and when it is to be released here:

_____

_____

_____

_____

_____

_____

_____

_____

Lessons / Modules that I have found to be particularly helpful or interesting:

_____

_____

_____

_____

_____

Course title: _____

Instructor name: _____

Date of purchase: _____ Amount Paid: _____

Email address used for purchase: _____

Date email confirmation was received: _____

Email confirmation sent from: _____

Order # from email confirmation: _____

Does course come with a satisfaction guarantee?   Yes / No   If yes,
when does guarantee expire? _____

Lifetime access to course material? Yes / No   If no, when does access
expire? _____

Log in URL: _____

User name: _____ Password: _____

Is any bonus content included with purchase?   Yes / No

If yes, list bonus content and when it is to be released here:

_____

_____

_____

_____

_____

_____

_____

_____

Lessons / Modules that I have found to be particularly helpful or interesting:

_____

_____

_____

_____

_____

Course title: _____

Instructor name: _____

Date of purchase: _____ Amount Paid: _____

Email address used for purchase: _____

Date email confirmation was received: _____

Email confirmation sent from: _____

Order # from email confirmation: _____

Does course come with a satisfaction guarantee?   Yes / No   If yes,

when does guarantee expire? _____

Lifetime access to course material? Yes / No   If no, when does access

expire? _____

Log in URL: _____

User name: _____ Password: _____

Is any bonus content included with purchase?   Yes / No

If yes, list bonus content and when it is to be released here:

_____

_____

_____

_____

_____

_____

_____

_____

Lessons / Modules that I have found to be particularly helpful or interesting:

_____

_____

_____

_____

_____

Course title: _____

Instructor name: _____

Date of purchase: _____ Amount Paid: _____

Email address used for purchase: _____

Date email confirmation was received: _____

Email confirmation sent from: _____

Order # from email confirmation: _____

Does course come with a satisfaction guarantee?   Yes / No   If yes,
when does guarantee expire? _____

Lifetime access to course material?   Yes / No   If no, when does access
expire? _____

Log in URL: _____

User name: _____ Password: _____

Is any bonus content included with purchase?   Yes / No

If yes, list bonus content and when it is to be released here:

_____

_____

_____

_____

_____

_____

_____

_____

Lessons / Modules that I have found to be particularly helpful or interesting:

_____

_____

_____

_____

_____

Course title: _____

Instructor name: _____

Date of purchase: _____ Amount Paid: _____

Email address used for purchase: _____

Date email confirmation was received: _____

Email confirmation sent from: _____

Order # from email confirmation: _____

Does course come with a satisfaction guarantee?　Yes　/　No　　If yes, when does guarantee expire? _____

Lifetime access to course material?　Yes　/　No　　If no, when does access expire? _____

Log in URL: _____

User name: _____ Password: _____

Is any bonus content included with purchase?　Yes　/　No

If yes, list bonus content and when it is to be released here:

_____

_____

_____

_____

_____

_____

_____

_____

Lessons / Modules that I have found to be particularly helpful or interesting:

_____

_____

_____

_____

_____

Course title: _____

Instructor name: _____

Date of purchase: _____ Amount Paid: _____

Email address used for purchase: _____

Date email confirmation was received: _____

Email confirmation sent from: _____

Order # from email confirmation: _____

Does course come with a satisfaction guarantee?   Yes / No   If yes, when does guarantee expire? _____

Lifetime access to course material?   Yes / No   If no, when does access expire? _____

Log in URL: _____

User name: _____ Password: _____

Is any bonus content included with purchase?   Yes / No

If yes, list bonus content and when it is to be released here:

_____

_____

_____

_____

_____

_____

_____

Lessons / Modules that I have found to be particularly helpful or interesting:

_____

_____

_____

_____

_____

Course title: _____

Instructor name: _____

Date of purchase: _____ Amount Paid: _____

Email address used for purchase: _____

Date email confirmation was received: _____

Email confirmation sent from: _____

Order # from email confirmation: _____

Does course come with a satisfaction guarantee?   Yes / No   If yes,

when does guarantee expire? _____

Lifetime access to course material? Yes / No   If no, when does access

expire? _____

Log in URL: _____

User name: _____ Password: _____

Is any bonus content included with purchase?   Yes / No

If yes, list bonus content and when it is to be released here:

_____

_____

_____

_____

_____

_____

_____

_____

Lessons / Modules that I have found to be particularly helpful or interesting:

_____

_____

_____

_____

_____

Course title: _____

Instructor name: _____

Date of purchase: _____ Amount Paid: _____

Email address used for purchase: _____

Date email confirmation was received: _____

Email confirmation sent from: _____

Order # from email confirmation: _____

Does course come with a satisfaction guarantee?   Yes / No   If yes,
when does guarantee expire? _____

Lifetime access to course material? Yes / No   If no, when does access
expire?   _____

Log in URL: _____

User name: _____ Password: _____

Is any bonus content included with purchase?   Yes / No

If yes, list bonus content and when it is to be released here:

_____

_____

_____

_____

_____

_____

_____

_____

Lessons / Modules that I have found to be particularly helpful or interesting:

_____

_____

_____

_____

_____

Course title: _____

Instructor name: _____

Date of purchase: _____ Amount Paid: _____

Email address used for purchase: _____

Date email confirmation was received: _____

Email confirmation sent from: _____

Order # from email confirmation: _____

Does course come with a satisfaction guarantee?   Yes / No   If yes,

when does guarantee expire? _____

Lifetime access to course material? Yes / No   If no, when does access

expire? _____

Log in URL: _____

User name: _____ Password: _____

Is any bonus content included with purchase?   Yes / No

If yes, list bonus content and when it is to be released here:

_____

_____

_____

_____

_____

_____

_____

_____

Lessons / Modules that I have found to be particularly helpful or interesting:

_____

_____

_____

_____

_____

Course title: _____

Instructor name: _____

Date of purchase: _____ Amount Paid: _____

Email address used for purchase: _____

Date email confirmation was received: _____

Email confirmation sent from: _____

Order # from email confirmation: _____

Does course come with a satisfaction guarantee?   Yes / No   If yes,
when does guarantee expire? _____

Lifetime access to course material? Yes / No   If no, when does access
expire? _____

Log in URL: _____

User name: _____ Password: _____

Is any bonus content included with purchase?   Yes / No

If yes, list bonus content and when it is to be released here:

_____

_____

_____

_____

_____

_____

_____

_____

Lessons / Modules that I have found to be particularly helpful or interesting:

_____

_____

_____

_____

_____

Course title: _____

Instructor name: _____

Date of purchase: _____ Amount Paid: _____

Email address used for purchase: _____

Date email confirmation was received: _____

Email confirmation sent from: _____

Order # from email confirmation: _____

Does course come with a satisfaction guarantee?   Yes / No   If yes,
when does guarantee expire? _____

Lifetime access to course material? Yes / No   If no, when does access
expire? _____

Log in URL: _____

User name: _____ Password: _____

Is any bonus content included with purchase?   Yes / No

If yes, list bonus content and when it is to be released here:

_____

_____

_____

_____

_____

_____

_____

_____

Lessons / Modules that I have found to be particularly helpful or interesting:

_____

_____

_____

_____

_____

Course title: _____

Instructor name: _____

Date of purchase: _____ Amount Paid: _____

Email address used for purchase: _____

Date email confirmation was received: _____

Email confirmation sent from: _____

Order # from email confirmation: _____

Does course come with a satisfaction guarantee?   Yes / No   If yes,
when does guarantee expire? _____

Lifetime access to course material?   Yes / No   If no, when does access
expire? _____

Log in URL: _____

User name: _____ Password: _____

Is any bonus content included with purchase?   Yes / No

If yes, list bonus content and when it is to be released here:

_____

_____

_____

_____

_____

_____

_____

_____

_____

Lessons / Modules that I have found to be particularly helpful or interesting:

_____

_____

_____

_____

_____

Course title: _____

Instructor name: _____

Date of purchase: _____ Amount Paid: _____

Email address used for purchase: _____

Date email confirmation was received: _____

Email confirmation sent from: _____

Order # from email confirmation: _____

Does course come with a satisfaction guarantee?   Yes / No   If yes, when does guarantee expire? _____

Lifetime access to course material? Yes / No   If no, when does access expire? _____

Log in URL: _____

User name: _____ Password: _____

Is any bonus content included with purchase?   Yes / No

If yes, list bonus content and when it is to be released here:

_____

_____

_____

_____

_____

_____

_____

_____

Lessons / Modules that I have found to be particularly helpful or interesting:

_____

_____

_____

_____

Course title: _____

Instructor name: _____

Date of purchase: _____ Amount Paid: _____

Email address used for purchase: _____

Date email confirmation was received: _____

Email confirmation sent from: _____

Order # from email confirmation: _____

Does course come with a satisfaction guarantee?   Yes / No   If yes,
when does guarantee expire? _____

Lifetime access to course material?   Yes / No   If no, when does access
expire? _____

Log in URL: _____

User name: _____ Password: _____

Is any bonus content included with purchase?   Yes / No

If yes, list bonus content and when it is to be released here:

_____

_____

_____

_____

_____

_____

_____

_____

Lessons / Modules that I have found to be particularly helpful or interesting:

_____

_____

_____

_____

_____

Course title: _____

Instructor name: _____

Date of purchase: _____ Amount Paid: _____

Email address used for purchase: _____

Date email confirmation was received: _____

Email confirmation sent from: _____

Order # from email confirmation: _____

Does course come with a satisfaction guarantee?   Yes / No   If yes,
when does guarantee expire? _____

Lifetime access to course material? Yes / No   If no, when does access
expire? _____

Log in URL: _____

User name: _____ Password: _____

Is any bonus content included with purchase?   Yes / No

If yes, list bonus content and when it is to be released here:

_____

_____

_____

_____

_____

_____

_____

_____

Lessons / Modules that I have found to be particularly helpful or interesting:

_____

_____

_____

_____

Course title: _____

Instructor name: _____

Date of purchase: _____ Amount Paid: _____

Email address used for purchase: _____

Date email confirmation was received: _____

Email confirmation sent from: _____

Order # from email confirmation: _____

Does course come with a satisfaction guarantee?   Yes / No   If yes, when does guarantee expire? _____

Lifetime access to course material? Yes / No   If no, when does access expire? _____

Log in URL: _____

User name: _____ Password: _____

Is any bonus content included with purchase?   Yes / No

If yes, list bonus content and when it is to be released here:

_____
_____
_____
_____
_____
_____
_____
_____

Lessons / Modules that I have found to be particularly helpful or interesting:

_____
_____
_____
_____
_____

Course title: _____

Instructor name: _____

Date of purchase: _____ Amount Paid: _____

Email address used for purchase: _____

Date email confirmation was received: _____

Email confirmation sent from: _____

Order # from email confirmation: _____

Does course come with a satisfaction guarantee?   Yes / No   If yes,

when does guarantee expire? _____

Lifetime access to course material? Yes / No   If no, when does access

expire? _____

Log in URL: _____

User name: _____ Password: _____

Is any bonus content included with purchase?   Yes / No

If yes, list bonus content and when it is to be released here:

_____

_____

_____

_____

_____

_____

_____

_____

_____

Lessons / Modules that I have found to be particularly helpful or interesting:

_____

_____

_____

_____

_____

Course title: _____

Instructor name: _____

Date of purchase: _____ Amount Paid: _____

Email address used for purchase: _____

Date email confirmation was received: _____

Email confirmation sent from: _____

Order # from email confirmation: _____

Does course come with a satisfaction guarantee?   Yes / No   If yes,
when does guarantee expire? _____

Lifetime access to course material?   Yes / No   If no, when does access
expire? _____

Log in URL: _____

User name: _____ Password: _____

Is any bonus content included with purchase?   Yes / No

If yes, list bonus content and when it is to be released here:

_____

_____

_____

_____

_____

_____

_____

_____

Lessons / Modules that I have found to be particularly helpful or interesting:

_____

_____

_____

_____

_____

Course title: _____

Instructor name: _____

Date of purchase: _____ Amount Paid: _____

Email address used for purchase: _____

Date email confirmation was received: _____

Email confirmation sent from: _____

Order # from email confirmation: _____

Does course come with a satisfaction guarantee?   Yes / No   If yes,
when does guarantee expire? _____

Lifetime access to course material? Yes / No   If no, when does access
expire? _____

Log in URL: _____

User name: _____ Password: _____

Is any bonus content included with purchase?   Yes / No

If yes, list bonus content and when it is to be released here:

_____

_____

_____

_____

_____

_____

_____

_____

Lessons / Modules that I have found to be particularly helpful or interesting:

_____

_____

_____

_____

_____

Course title: _____

Instructor name: _____

Date of purchase: _____ Amount Paid: _____

Email address used for purchase: _____

Date email confirmation was received: _____

Email confirmation sent from: _____

Order # from email confirmation: _____

Does course come with a satisfaction guarantee?   Yes / No   If yes,
when does guarantee expire? _____

Lifetime access to course material? Yes / No   If no, when does access
expire? _____

Log in URL: _____

User name: _____ Password: _____

Is any bonus content included with purchase?   Yes / No

If yes, list bonus content and when it is to be released here:

_____

_____

_____

_____

_____

_____

_____

_____

_____

Lessons / Modules that I have found to be particularly helpful or interesting:

_____

_____

_____

_____

_____

Course title: _____

Instructor name: _____

Date of purchase: _____ Amount Paid: _____

Email address used for purchase: _____

Date email confirmation was received: _____

Email confirmation sent from: _____

Order # from email confirmation: _____

Does course come with a satisfaction guarantee? Yes / No If yes,
when does guarantee expire? _____

Lifetime access to course material? Yes / No If no, when does access
expire? _____

Log in URL: _____

User name: _____ Password: _____

Is any bonus content included with purchase? Yes / No

If yes, list bonus content and when it is to be released here:

_____

_____

_____

_____

_____

_____

_____

_____

Lessons / Modules that I have found to be particularly helpful or interesting:

_____

_____

_____

_____

_____

Course title: _____

Instructor name: _____

Date of purchase: _____ Amount Paid: _____

Email address used for purchase: _____

Date email confirmation was received: _____

Email confirmation sent from: _____

Order # from email confirmation: _____

Does course come with a satisfaction guarantee?   Yes / No   If yes, when does guarantee expire? _____

Lifetime access to course material? Yes / No   If no, when does access expire? _____

Log in URL: _____

User name: _____ Password: _____

Is any bonus content included with purchase?   Yes / No

If yes, list bonus content and when it is to be released here:

_____

_____

_____

_____

_____

_____

_____

_____

Lessons / Modules that I have found to be particularly helpful or interesting:

_____

_____

_____

_____

_____

Course title: _____

Instructor name: _____

Date of purchase: _____ Amount Paid: _____

Email address used for purchase: _____

Date email confirmation was received: _____

Email confirmation sent from: _____

Order # from email confirmation: _____

Does course come with a satisfaction guarantee?   Yes / No   If yes,

when does guarantee expire? _____

Lifetime access to course material?   Yes / No   If no, when does access

expire?   _____

Log in URL: _____

User name: _____ Password: _____

Is any bonus content included with purchase?   Yes / No

If yes, list bonus content and when it is to be released here:

_____

_____

_____

_____

_____

_____

_____

_____

Lessons / Modules that I have found to be particularly helpful or interesting:

_____

_____

_____

_____

Course title: _____

Instructor name: _____

Date of purchase: _____ Amount Paid: _____

Email address used for purchase: _____

Date email confirmation was received: _____

Email confirmation sent from: _____

Order # from email confirmation: _____

Does course come with a satisfaction guarantee?   Yes / No   If yes, when does guarantee expire? _____

Lifetime access to course material?   Yes / No   If no, when does access expire? _____

Log in URL: _____

User name: _____ Password: _____

Is any bonus content included with purchase?   Yes / No

If yes, list bonus content and when it is to be released here:

_____

_____

_____

_____

_____

_____

_____

_____

Lessons / Modules that I have found to be particularly helpful or interesting:

_____

_____

_____

_____

_____

Course title: _____

Instructor name: _____

Date of purchase: _____ Amount Paid: _____

Email address used for purchase: _____

Date email confirmation was received: _____

Email confirmation sent from: _____

Order # from email confirmation: _____

Does course come with a satisfaction guarantee?   Yes / No   If yes, when does guarantee expire? _____

Lifetime access to course material? Yes / No   If no, when does access expire?   _____

Log in URL: _____

User name: _____ Password: _____

Is any bonus content included with purchase?   Yes / No

If yes, list bonus content and when it is to be released here:

_____

_____

_____

_____

_____

_____

_____

_____

Lessons / Modules that I have found to be particularly helpful or interesting:

_____

_____

_____

_____

Course title: _____

Instructor name: _____

Date of purchase: _____ Amount Paid: _____

Email address used for purchase: _____

Date email confirmation was received: _____

Email confirmation sent from: _____

Order # from email confirmation: _____

Does course come with a satisfaction guarantee?   Yes / No   If yes, when does guarantee expire? _____

Lifetime access to course material? Yes / No   If no, when does access expire? _____

Log in URL: _____

User name: _____ Password: _____

Is any bonus content included with purchase?   Yes / No

If yes, list bonus content and when it is to be released here:

_____

_____

_____

_____

_____

_____

_____

_____

Lessons / Modules that I have found to be particularly helpful or interesting:

_____

_____

_____

_____

_____

Course title: _____

Instructor name: _____

Date of purchase: _____ Amount Paid: _____

Email address used for purchase: _____

Date email confirmation was received: _____

Email confirmation sent from: _____

Order # from email confirmation: _____

Does course come with a satisfaction guarantee?   Yes / No   If yes,
when does guarantee expire? _____

Lifetime access to course material? Yes / No   If no, when does access
expire? _____

Log in URL: _____

User name: _____ Password: _____

Is any bonus content included with purchase?   Yes / No

If yes, list bonus content and when it is to be released here:

_____

_____

_____

_____

_____

_____

_____

_____

Lessons / Modules that I have found to be particularly helpful or interesting:

_____

_____

_____

_____

_____

Course title: _____

Instructor name: _____

Date of purchase: _____ Amount Paid: _____

Email address used for purchase: _____

Date email confirmation was received: _____

Email confirmation sent from: _____

Order # from email confirmation: _____

Does course come with a satisfaction guarantee?   Yes / No   If yes,

when does guarantee expire? _____

Lifetime access to course material? Yes / No   If no, when does access

expire?   _____

Log in URL: _____

User name: _____ Password: _____

Is any bonus content included with purchase?   Yes / No

If yes, list bonus content and when it is to be released here:

_____

_____

_____

_____

_____

_____

_____

_____

Lessons / Modules that I have found to be particularly helpful or interesting:

_____

_____

_____

_____

_____

Course title: _____

Instructor name: _____

Date of purchase: _____ Amount Paid: _____

Email address used for purchase: _____

Date email confirmation was received: _____

Email confirmation sent from: _____

Order # from email confirmation: _____

Does course come with a satisfaction guarantee?   Yes / No   If yes, when does guarantee expire? _____

Lifetime access to course material? Yes / No   If no, when does access expire? _____

Log in URL: _____

User name: _____ Password: _____

Is any bonus content included with purchase?   Yes / No

If yes, list bonus content and when it is to be released here:

_____

_____

_____

_____

_____

_____

_____

_____

Lessons / Modules that I have found to be particularly helpful or interesting:

_____

_____

_____

_____

_____

Course title: _____

Instructor name: _____

Date of purchase: _____ Amount Paid: _____

Email address used for purchase: _____

Date email confirmation was received: _____

Email confirmation sent from: _____

Order # from email confirmation: _____

Does course come with a satisfaction guarantee?   Yes / No   If yes, when does guarantee expire? _____

Lifetime access to course material? Yes / No   If no, when does access expire? _____

Log in URL: _____

User name: _____ Password: _____

Is any bonus content included with purchase?   Yes / No

If yes, list bonus content and when it is to be released here:

_____

_____

_____

_____

_____

_____

_____

_____

Lessons / Modules that I have found to be particularly helpful or interesting:

_____

_____

_____

_____

_____

Course title: _____

Instructor name: _____

Date of purchase: _____ Amount Paid: _____

Email address used for purchase: _____

Date email confirmation was received: _____

Email confirmation sent from: _____

Order # from email confirmation: _____

Does course come with a satisfaction guarantee?   Yes / No   If yes,
when does guarantee expire? _____

Lifetime access to course material? Yes / No   If no, when does access
expire? _____

Log in URL: _____

User name: _____ Password: _____

Is any bonus content included with purchase?   Yes / No

If yes, list bonus content and when it is to be released here:

_____

_____

_____

_____

_____

_____

_____

_____

_____

Lessons / Modules that I have found to be particularly helpful or interesting:

_____

_____

_____

_____

_____

Course title: _____

Instructor name: _____

Date of purchase: _____ Amount Paid: _____

Email address used for purchase: _____

Date email confirmation was received: _____

Email confirmation sent from: _____

Order # from email confirmation: _____

Does course come with a satisfaction guarantee?   Yes / No   If yes, when does guarantee expire? _____

Lifetime access to course material? Yes / No   If no, when does access expire? _____

Log in URL: _____

User name: _____ Password: _____

Is any bonus content included with purchase?   Yes / No

If yes, list bonus content and when it is to be released here:

_____

_____

_____

_____

_____

_____

_____

_____

Lessons / Modules that I have found to be particularly helpful or interesting:

_____

_____

_____

_____

_____

Course title: _____

Instructor name: _____

Date of purchase: _____ Amount Paid: _____

Email address used for purchase: _____

Date email confirmation was received: _____

Email confirmation sent from: _____

Order # from email confirmation: _____

Does course come with a satisfaction guarantee?   Yes / No   If yes, when does guarantee expire? _____

Lifetime access to course material? Yes / No   If no, when does access expire? _____

Log in URL: _____

User name: _____ Password: _____

Is any bonus content included with purchase?   Yes / No

If yes, list bonus content and when it is to be released here:

_____

_____

_____

_____

_____

_____

_____

_____

Lessons / Modules that I have found to be particularly helpful or interesting:

_____

_____

_____

_____

_____

Course title: _____

Instructor name: _____

Date of purchase: _____ Amount Paid: _____

Email address used for purchase: _____

Date email confirmation was received: _____

Email confirmation sent from: _____

Order # from email confirmation: _____

Does course come with a satisfaction guarantee?   Yes / No   If yes, when does guarantee expire? _____

Lifetime access to course material? Yes / No   If no, when does access expire? _____

Log in URL: _____

User name: _____ Password: _____

Is any bonus content included with purchase?   Yes / No

If yes, list bonus content and when it is to be released here:

_____
_____
_____
_____
_____
_____
_____
_____
_____

Lessons / Modules that I have found to be particularly helpful or interesting:

_____
_____
_____
_____
_____

Course title: _____

Instructor name: _____

Date of purchase: _____ Amount Paid: _____

Email address used for purchase: _____

Date email confirmation was received: _____

Email confirmation sent from: _____

Order # from email confirmation: _____

Does course come with a satisfaction guarantee?   Yes / No   If yes, when does guarantee expire? _____

Lifetime access to course material? Yes / No   If no, when does access expire? _____

Log in URL: _____

User name: _____ Password: _____

Is any bonus content included with purchase?   Yes / No

If yes, list bonus content and when it is to be released here:

_____

_____

_____

_____

_____

_____

_____

_____

Lessons / Modules that I have found to be particularly helpful or interesting:

_____

_____

_____

_____

_____

Course title: _____

Instructor name: _____

Date of purchase: _____ Amount Paid: _____

Email address used for purchase: _____

Date email confirmation was received: _____

Email confirmation sent from: _____

Order # from email confirmation: _____

Does course come with a satisfaction guarantee?   Yes / No   If yes,
when does guarantee expire? _____

Lifetime access to course material? Yes / No   If no, when does access
expire? _____

Log in URL: _____

User name: _____ Password: _____

Is any bonus content included with purchase?   Yes / No

If yes, list bonus content and when it is to be released here:

_____
_____
_____
_____
_____
_____
_____
_____
_____

Lessons / Modules that I have found to be particularly helpful or interesting:

_____
_____
_____
_____
_____

Course title: _____

Instructor name: _____

Date of purchase: _____ Amount Paid: _____

Email address used for purchase: _____

Date email confirmation was received: _____

Email confirmation sent from: _____

Order # from email confirmation: _____

Does course come with a satisfaction guarantee?   Yes / No   If yes, when does guarantee expire? _____

Lifetime access to course material? Yes / No   If no, when does access expire? _____

Log in URL: _____

User name: _____ Password: _____

Is any bonus content included with purchase?   Yes / No

If yes, list bonus content and when it is to be released here:

_____
_____
_____
_____
_____
_____
_____
_____

Lessons / Modules that I have found to be particularly helpful or interesting:

_____
_____
_____
_____

Course title: _____

Instructor name: _____

Date of purchase: _____ Amount Paid: _____

Email address used for purchase: _____

Date email confirmation was received: _____

Email confirmation sent from: _____

Order # from email confirmation: _____

Does course come with a satisfaction guarantee?   Yes / No   If yes, when does guarantee expire? _____

Lifetime access to course material?   Yes / No   If no, when does access expire? _____

Log in URL: _____

User name: _____ Password: _____

Is any bonus content included with purchase?   Yes / No

If yes, list bonus content and when it is to be released here:

_____
_____
_____
_____
_____
_____
_____
_____

Lessons / Modules that I have found to be particularly helpful or interesting:

_____
_____
_____
_____
_____

Course title: _____

Instructor name: _____

Date of purchase: _____ Amount Paid: _____

Email address used for purchase: _____

Date email confirmation was received: _____

Email confirmation sent from: _____

Order # from email confirmation: _____

Does course come with a satisfaction guarantee?   Yes / No   If yes,

when does guarantee expire? _____

Lifetime access to course material?   Yes / No   If no, when does access

expire? _____

Log in URL: _____

User name: _____ Password: _____

Is any bonus content included with purchase?   Yes / No

If yes, list bonus content and when it is to be released here:

_____

_____

_____

_____

_____

_____

_____

_____

_____

Lessons / Modules that I have found to be particularly helpful or interesting:

_____

_____

_____

_____

_____

Course title: _____

Instructor name: _____

Date of purchase: _____ Amount Paid: _____

Email address used for purchase: _____

Date email confirmation was received: _____

Email confirmation sent from: _____

Order # from email confirmation: _____

Does course come with a satisfaction guarantee? Yes / No If yes, when does guarantee expire? _____

Lifetime access to course material? Yes / No If no, when does access expire? _____

Log in URL: _____

User name: _____ Password: _____

Is any bonus content included with purchase? Yes / No

If yes, list bonus content and when it is to be released here:

_____

_____

_____

_____

_____

_____

_____

_____

_____

Lessons / Modules that I have found to be particularly helpful or interesting:

_____

_____

_____

_____

_____

Course title: _____

Instructor name: _____

Date of purchase: _____ Amount Paid: _____

Email address used for purchase: _____

Date email confirmation was received: _____

Email confirmation sent from: _____

Order # from email confirmation: _____

Does course come with a satisfaction guarantee? Yes / No If yes,

when does guarantee expire? _____

Lifetime access to course material? Yes / No If no, when does access

expire? _____

Log in URL: _____

User name: _____ Password: _____

Is any bonus content included with purchase? Yes / No

If yes, list bonus content and when it is to be released here:

_____

_____

_____

_____

_____

_____

_____

_____

Lessons / Modules that I have found to be particularly helpful or interesting:

_____

_____

_____

_____

_____

Course title: _____

Instructor name: _____

Date of purchase: _____ Amount Paid: _____

Email address used for purchase: _____

Date email confirmation was received: _____

Email confirmation sent from: _____

Order # from email confirmation: _____

Does course come with a satisfaction guarantee?   Yes / No   If yes, when does guarantee expire? _____

Lifetime access to course material? Yes / No   If no, when does access expire? _____

Log in URL: _____

User name: _____ Password: _____

Is any bonus content included with purchase?   Yes / No

If yes, list bonus content and when it is to be released here:

_____

_____

_____

_____

_____

_____

_____

_____

_____

Lessons / Modules that I have found to be particularly helpful or interesting:

_____

_____

_____

_____

_____

Course title: _____

Instructor name: _____

Date of purchase: _____ Amount Paid: _____

Email address used for purchase: _____

Date email confirmation was received: _____

Email confirmation sent from: _____

Order # from email confirmation: _____

Does course come with a satisfaction guarantee?   Yes / No   If yes, when does guarantee expire? _____

Lifetime access to course material? Yes / No   If no, when does access expire? _____

Log in URL: _____

User name: _____ Password: _____

Is any bonus content included with purchase?   Yes / No

If yes, list bonus content and when it is to be released here:

_____

_____

_____

_____

_____

_____

_____

_____

_____

Lessons / Modules that I have found to be particularly helpful or interesting:

_____

_____

_____

_____

_____

Course title: _____

Instructor name: _____

Date of purchase: _____ Amount Paid: _____

Email address used for purchase: _____

Date email confirmation was received: _____

Email confirmation sent from: _____

Order # from email confirmation: _____

Does course come with a satisfaction guarantee?   Yes / No   If yes,
when does guarantee expire? _____

Lifetime access to course material?   Yes / No   If no, when does access
expire? _____

Log in URL: _____

User name: _____ Password: _____

Is any bonus content included with purchase?   Yes / No

If yes, list bonus content and when it is to be released here:

_____

_____

_____

_____

_____

_____

_____

_____

_____

Lessons / Modules that I have found to be particularly helpful or interesting:

_____

_____

_____

_____

_____

Course title: _____

Instructor name: _____

Date of purchase: _____ Amount Paid: _____

Email address used for purchase: _____

Date email confirmation was received: _____

Email confirmation sent from: _____

Order # from email confirmation: _____

Does course come with a satisfaction guarantee?   Yes / No   If yes,

when does guarantee expire? _____

Lifetime access to course material? Yes / No   If no, when does access

expire? _____

Log in URL: _____

User name: _____ Password: _____

Is any bonus content included with purchase?   Yes / No

If yes, list bonus content and when it is to be released here:

_____
_____
_____
_____
_____
_____
_____
_____
_____

Lessons / Modules that I have found to be particularly helpful or interesting:

_____
_____
_____
_____
_____

Course title: _____

Instructor name: _____

Date of purchase: _____ Amount Paid: _____

Email address used for purchase: _____

Date email confirmation was received: _____

Email confirmation sent from: _____

Order # from email confirmation: _____

Does course come with a satisfaction guarantee?   Yes / No   If yes, when does guarantee expire? _____

Lifetime access to course material? Yes / No   If no, when does access expire? _____

Log in URL: _____

User name: _____ Password: _____

Is any bonus content included with purchase?   Yes / No

If yes, list bonus content and when it is to be released here:

_____

_____

_____

_____

_____

_____

_____

_____

Lessons / Modules that I have found to be particularly helpful or interesting:

_____

_____

_____

_____

_____

Course title: _____

Instructor name: _____

Date of purchase: _____ Amount Paid: _____

Email address used for purchase: _____

Date email confirmation was received: _____

Email confirmation sent from: _____

Order # from email confirmation: _____

Does course come with a satisfaction guarantee? Yes / No If yes,

when does guarantee expire? _____

Lifetime access to course material? Yes / No If no, when does access

expire? _____

Log in URL: _____

User name: _____ Password: _____

Is any bonus content included with purchase? Yes / No

If yes, list bonus content and when it is to be released here:

_____

_____

_____

_____

_____

_____

_____

_____

Lessons / Modules that I have found to be particularly helpful or interesting:

_____

_____

_____

_____

_____

Course title: _____

Instructor name: _____

Date of purchase: _____ Amount Paid: _____

Email address used for purchase: _____

Date email confirmation was received: _____

Email confirmation sent from: _____

Order # from email confirmation: _____

Does course come with a satisfaction guarantee?   Yes / No   If yes, when does guarantee expire? _____

Lifetime access to course material?   Yes / No   If no, when does access expire? _____

Log in URL: _____

User name: _____ Password: _____

Is any bonus content included with purchase?   Yes / No

If yes, list bonus content and when it is to be released here:

_____
_____
_____
_____
_____
_____
_____
_____
_____

Lessons / Modules that I have found to be particularly helpful or interesting:

_____
_____
_____
_____
_____

Course title: _____

Instructor name: _____

Date of purchase: _____ Amount Paid: _____

Email address used for purchase: _____

Date email confirmation was received: _____

Email confirmation sent from: _____

Order # from email confirmation: _____

Does course come with a satisfaction guarantee?   Yes / No   If yes, when does guarantee expire? _____

Lifetime access to course material? Yes / No   If no, when does access expire? _____

Log in URL: _____

User name: _____ Password: _____

Is any bonus content included with purchase?   Yes / No

If yes, list bonus content and when it is to be released here:

_____

_____

_____

_____

_____

_____

_____

_____

Lessons / Modules that I have found to be particularly helpful or interesting:

_____

_____

_____

_____

_____

Course title: _____

Instructor name: _____

Date of purchase: _____ Amount Paid: _____

Email address used for purchase: _____

Date email confirmation was received: _____

Email confirmation sent from: _____

Order # from email confirmation: _____

Does course come with a satisfaction guarantee?   Yes / No   If yes, when does guarantee expire? _____

Lifetime access to course material?   Yes / No   If no, when does access expire? _____

Log in URL: _____

User name: _____ Password: _____

Is any bonus content included with purchase?   Yes / No

If yes, list bonus content and when it is to be released here:

_____

_____

_____

_____

_____

_____

_____

_____

Lessons / Modules that I have found to be particularly helpful or interesting:

_____

_____

_____

_____

_____

Course title: _____

Instructor name: _____

Date of purchase: _____ Amount Paid: _____

Email address used for purchase: _____

Date email confirmation was received: _____

Email confirmation sent from: _____

Order # from email confirmation: _____

Does course come with a satisfaction guarantee?   Yes / No   If yes, when does guarantee expire? _____

Lifetime access to course material? Yes / No   If no, when does access expire? _____

Log in URL: _____

User name: _____ Password: _____

Is any bonus content included with purchase?   Yes / No

If yes, list bonus content and when it is to be released here:

_____

_____

_____

_____

_____

_____

_____

_____

Lessons / Modules that I have found to be particularly helpful or interesting:

_____

_____

_____

_____

_____

Course title: _____

Instructor name: _____

Date of purchase: _____ Amount Paid: _____

Email address used for purchase: _____

Date email confirmation was received: _____

Email confirmation sent from: _____

Order # from email confirmation: _____

Does course come with a satisfaction guarantee? Yes / No If yes, when does guarantee expire? _____

Lifetime access to course material? Yes / No If no, when does access expire? _____

Log in URL: _____

User name: _____ Password: _____

Is any bonus content included with purchase? Yes / No

If yes, list bonus content and when it is to be released here:

_____

_____

_____

_____

_____

_____

_____

_____

_____

Lessons / Modules that I have found to be particularly helpful or interesting:

_____

_____

_____

_____

_____

Course title: _____

Instructor name: _____

Date of purchase: _____ Amount Paid: _____

Email address used for purchase: _____

Date email confirmation was received: _____

Email confirmation sent from: _____

Order # from email confirmation: _____

Does course come with a satisfaction guarantee?   Yes / No   If yes,

when does guarantee expire? _____

Lifetime access to course material? Yes / No   If no, when does access

expire? _____

Log in URL: _____

User name: _____ Password: _____

Is any bonus content included with purchase?   Yes / No

If yes, list bonus content and when it is to be released here:

_____

_____

_____

_____

_____

_____

_____

_____

Lessons / Modules that I have found to be particularly helpful or interesting:

_____

_____

_____

_____

_____

Course title: _____

Instructor name: _____

Date of purchase: _____ Amount Paid: _____

Email address used for purchase: _____

Date email confirmation was received: _____

Email confirmation sent from: _____

Order # from email confirmation: _____

Does course come with a satisfaction guarantee?   Yes / No   If yes,
when does guarantee expire? _____

Lifetime access to course material? Yes / No   If no, when does access
expire? _____

Log in URL: _____

User name: _____ Password: _____

Is any bonus content included with purchase?   Yes / No

If yes, list bonus content and when it is to be released here:

_____

_____

_____

_____

_____

_____

_____

_____

Lessons / Modules that I have found to be particularly helpful or interesting:

_____

_____

_____

_____

_____

Course title: _____

Instructor name: _____

Date of purchase: _____ Amount Paid: _____

Email address used for purchase: _____

Date email confirmation was received: _____

Email confirmation sent from: _____

Order # from email confirmation: _____

Does course come with a satisfaction guarantee?   Yes / No   If yes, when does guarantee expire? _____

Lifetime access to course material? Yes / No   If no, when does access expire? _____

Log in URL: _____

User name: _____ Password: _____

Is any bonus content included with purchase?   Yes / No

If yes, list bonus content and when it is to be released here:

_____

_____

_____

_____

_____

_____

_____

_____

Lessons / Modules that I have found to be particularly helpful or interesting:

_____

_____

_____

_____

_____

Course title: _____

Instructor name: _____

Date of purchase: _____ Amount Paid: _____

Email address used for purchase: _____

Date email confirmation was received: _____

Email confirmation sent from: _____

Order # from email confirmation: _____

Does course come with a satisfaction guarantee?   Yes / No   If yes,
when does guarantee expire? _____

Lifetime access to course material? Yes / No   If no, when does access
expire?   _____

Log in URL: _____

User name: _____ Password: _____

Is any bonus content included with purchase?   Yes / No

If yes, list bonus content and when it is to be released here:

_____

_____

_____

_____

_____

_____

_____

_____

Lessons / Modules that I have found to be particularly helpful or interesting:

_____

_____

_____

_____

_____

Course title: _____

Instructor name: _____

Date of purchase: _____ Amount Paid: _____

Email address used for purchase: _____

Date email confirmation was received: _____

Email confirmation sent from: _____

Order # from email confirmation: _____

Does course come with a satisfaction guarantee?   Yes / No   If yes,

when does guarantee expire? _____

Lifetime access to course material?   Yes / No   If no, when does access

expire? _____

Log in URL: _____

User name: _____ Password: _____

Is any bonus content included with purchase?   Yes / No

If yes, list bonus content and when it is to be released here:

_____

_____

_____

_____

_____

_____

_____

_____

_____

Lessons / Modules that I have found to be particularly helpful or interesting:

_____

_____

_____

_____

_____

Course title: _____

Instructor name: _____

Date of purchase: _____ Amount Paid: _____

Email address used for purchase: _____

Date email confirmation was received: _____

Email confirmation sent from: _____

Order # from email confirmation: _____

Does course come with a satisfaction guarantee?   Yes / No   If yes,
when does guarantee expire? _____

Lifetime access to course material? Yes / No   If no, when does access
expire? _____

Log in URL: _____

User name: _____ Password: _____

Is any bonus content included with purchase?   Yes / No

If yes, list bonus content and when it is to be released here:

_____

_____

_____

_____

_____

_____

_____

_____

Lessons / Modules that I have found to be particularly helpful or interesting:

_____

_____

_____

_____

_____

Course title: _____

Instructor name: _____

Date of purchase: _____ Amount Paid: _____

Email address used for purchase: _____

Date email confirmation was received: _____

Email confirmation sent from: _____

Order # from email confirmation: _____

Does course come with a satisfaction guarantee?   Yes / No   If yes,

when does guarantee expire? _____

Lifetime access to course material? Yes / No   If no, when does access

expire? _____

Log in URL: _____

User name: _____ Password: _____

Is any bonus content included with purchase?   Yes / No

If yes, list bonus content and when it is to be released here:

_____

_____

_____

_____

_____

_____

_____

_____

_____

Lessons / Modules that I have found to be particularly helpful or interesting:

_____

_____

_____

_____

_____

Course title: _____

Instructor name: _____

Date of purchase: _____ Amount Paid: _____

Email address used for purchase: _____

Date email confirmation was received: _____

Email confirmation sent from: _____

Order # from email confirmation: _____

Does course come with a satisfaction guarantee?   Yes / No   If yes,
when does guarantee expire? _____

Lifetime access to course material? Yes / No   If no, when does access
expire? _____

Log in URL: _____

User name: _____ Password: _____

Is any bonus content included with purchase?   Yes / No

If yes, list bonus content and when it is to be released here:

_____

_____

_____

_____

_____

_____

_____

_____

Lessons / Modules that I have found to be particularly helpful or interesting:

_____

_____

_____

_____

_____

Course title: _____

Instructor name: _____

Date of purchase: _____ Amount Paid: _____

Email address used for purchase: _____

Date email confirmation was received: _____

Email confirmation sent from: _____

Order # from email confirmation: _____

Does course come with a satisfaction guarantee?   Yes / No   If yes,

when does guarantee expire? _____

Lifetime access to course material? Yes / No   If no, when does access

expire? _____

Log in URL: _____

User name: _____ Password: _____

Is any bonus content included with purchase?   Yes / No

If yes, list bonus content and when it is to be released here:

_____
_____
_____
_____
_____
_____
_____
_____
_____

Lessons / Modules that I have found to be particularly helpful or interesting:

_____
_____
_____
_____
_____

Course title: _____

Instructor name: _____

Date of purchase: _____ Amount Paid: _____

Email address used for purchase: _____

Date email confirmation was received: _____

Email confirmation sent from: _____

Order # from email confirmation: _____

Does course come with a satisfaction guarantee?   Yes / No   If yes,
when does guarantee expire? _____

Lifetime access to course material? Yes / No   If no, when does access
expire? _____

Log in URL: _____

User name: _____ Password: _____

Is any bonus content included with purchase?   Yes / No

If yes, list bonus content and when it is to be released here:

_____

_____

_____

_____

_____

_____

_____

_____

_____

Lessons / Modules that I have found to be particularly helpful or interesting:

_____

_____

_____

_____

_____

Course title: _____

Instructor name: _____

Date of purchase: _____ Amount Paid: _____

Email address used for purchase: _____

Date email confirmation was received: _____

Email confirmation sent from: _____

Order # from email confirmation: _____

Does course come with a satisfaction guarantee?   Yes / No   If yes,

when does guarantee expire? _____

Lifetime access to course material? Yes / No   If no, when does access

expire? _____

Log in URL: _____

User name: _____ Password: _____

Is any bonus content included with purchase?   Yes / No

If yes, list bonus content and when it is to be released here:

_____

_____

_____

_____

_____

_____

_____

_____

Lessons / Modules that I have found to be particularly helpful or interesting:

_____

_____

_____

_____

_____

Course title: _____

Instructor name: _____

Date of purchase: _____ Amount Paid: _____

Email address used for purchase: _____

Date email confirmation was received: _____

Email confirmation sent from: _____

Order # from email confirmation: _____

Does course come with a satisfaction guarantee?   Yes / No   If yes, when does guarantee expire? _____

Lifetime access to course material?   Yes / No   If no, when does access expire? _____

Log in URL: _____

User name: _____ Password: _____

Is any bonus content included with purchase?   Yes / No

If yes, list bonus content and when it is to be released here:

_____
_____
_____
_____
_____
_____
_____
_____
_____

Lessons / Modules that I have found to be particularly helpful or interesting:

_____
_____
_____
_____
_____

Course title: _____

Instructor name: _____

Date of purchase: _____ Amount Paid: _____

Email address used for purchase: _____

Date email confirmation was received: _____

Email confirmation sent from: _____

Order # from email confirmation: _____

Does course come with a satisfaction guarantee?   Yes / No   If yes,

when does guarantee expire? _____

Lifetime access to course material? Yes / No   If no, when does access

expire? _____

Log in URL: _____

User name: _____ Password: _____

Is any bonus content included with purchase?   Yes / No

If yes, list bonus content and when it is to be released here:

_____

_____

_____

_____

_____

_____

_____

_____

Lessons / Modules that I have found to be particularly helpful or interesting:

_____

_____

_____

_____

_____

Course title: _____

Instructor name: _____

Date of purchase: _____ Amount Paid: _____

Email address used for purchase: _____

Date email confirmation was received: _____

Email confirmation sent from: _____

Order # from email confirmation: _____

Does course come with a satisfaction guarantee?   Yes / No   If yes,

when does guarantee expire? _____

Lifetime access to course material? Yes / No   If no, when does access

expire? _____

Log in URL: _____

User name: _____ Password: _____

Is any bonus content included with purchase?   Yes / No

If yes, list bonus content and when it is to be released here:

_____

_____

_____

_____

_____

_____

_____

_____

Lessons / Modules that I have found to be particularly helpful or interesting:

_____

_____

_____

_____

_____

Course title: _____

Instructor name: _____

Date of purchase: _____ Amount Paid: _____

Email address used for purchase: _____

Date email confirmation was received: _____

Email confirmation sent from: _____

Order # from email confirmation: _____

Does course come with a satisfaction guarantee? Yes / No If yes,

when does guarantee expire? _____

Lifetime access to course material? Yes / No If no, when does access

expire? _____

Log in URL: _____

User name: _____ Password: _____

Is any bonus content included with purchase? Yes / No

If yes, list bonus content and when it is to be released here:

_____

_____

_____

_____

_____

_____

_____

_____

Lessons / Modules that I have found to be particularly helpful or interesting:

_____

_____

_____

_____

_____

Course title: _____

Instructor name: _____

Date of purchase: _____ Amount Paid: _____

Email address used for purchase: _____

Date email confirmation was received: _____

Email confirmation sent from: _____

Order # from email confirmation: _____

Does course come with a satisfaction guarantee?   Yes / No   If yes,

when does guarantee expire? _____

Lifetime access to course material? Yes / No   If no, when does access

expire? _____

Log in URL: _____

User name: _____ Password: _____

Is any bonus content included with purchase?   Yes / No

If yes, list bonus content and when it is to be released here:

_____

_____

_____

_____

_____

_____

_____

_____

Lessons / Modules that I have found to be particularly helpful or interesting:

_____

_____

_____

_____

_____

Course title: _____

Instructor name: _____

Date of purchase: _____ Amount Paid: _____

Email address used for purchase: _____

Date email confirmation was received: _____

Email confirmation sent from: _____

Order # from email confirmation: _____

Does course come with a satisfaction guarantee? Yes / No   If yes, when does guarantee expire? _____

Lifetime access to course material? Yes / No   If no, when does access expire? _____

Log in URL: _____

User name: _____ Password: _____

Is any bonus content included with purchase? Yes / No

If yes, list bonus content and when it is to be released here:

_____
_____
_____
_____
_____
_____
_____
_____
_____

Lessons / Modules that I have found to be particularly helpful or interesting:

_____
_____
_____
_____
_____

Course title: _____

Instructor name: _____

Date of purchase: _____ Amount Paid: _____

Email address used for purchase: _____

Date email confirmation was received: _____

Email confirmation sent from: _____

Order # from email confirmation: _____

Does course come with a satisfaction guarantee?   Yes / No   If yes,
when does guarantee expire? _____

Lifetime access to course material? Yes / No   If no, when does access
expire? _____

Log in URL: _____

User name: _____ Password: _____

Is any bonus content included with purchase?   Yes / No

If yes, list bonus content and when it is to be released here:

_____
_____
_____
_____
_____
_____
_____
_____

Lessons / Modules that I have found to be particularly helpful or interesting:

_____
_____
_____
_____
_____

Course title: _____

Instructor name: _____

Date of purchase: _____ Amount Paid: _____

Email address used for purchase: _____

Date email confirmation was received: _____

Email confirmation sent from: _____

Order # from email confirmation: _____

Does course come with a satisfaction guarantee?   Yes / No   If yes,

when does guarantee expire? _____

Lifetime access to course material? Yes / No   If no, when does access

expire? _____

Log in URL: _____

User name: _____ Password: _____

Is any bonus content included with purchase?   Yes / No

If yes, list bonus content and when it is to be released here:

_____

_____

_____

_____

_____

_____

_____

_____

Lessons / Modules that I have found to be particularly helpful or interesting:

_____

_____

_____

_____

_____

Course title: _____

Instructor name: _____

Date of purchase: _____ Amount Paid: _____

Email address used for purchase: _____

Date email confirmation was received: _____

Email confirmation sent from: _____

Order # from email confirmation: _____

Does course come with a satisfaction guarantee?   Yes / No   If yes,
when does guarantee expire? _____

Lifetime access to course material? Yes / No   If no, when does access
expire? _____

Log in URL: _____

User name: _____ Password: _____

Is any bonus content included with purchase?   Yes / No

If yes, list bonus content and when it is to be released here:

_____

_____

_____

_____

_____

_____

_____

_____

_____

Lessons / Modules that I have found to be particularly helpful or interesting:

_____

_____

_____

_____

_____

Course title: _____

Instructor name: _____

Date of purchase: _____ Amount Paid: _____

Email address used for purchase: _____

Date email confirmation was received: _____

Email confirmation sent from: _____

Order # from email confirmation: _____

Does course come with a satisfaction guarantee?   Yes / No   If yes,
when does guarantee expire? _____

Lifetime access to course material? Yes / No   If no, when does access
expire? _____

Log in URL: _____

User name: _____ Password: _____

Is any bonus content included with purchase?   Yes / No

If yes, list bonus content and when it is to be released here:

_____
_____
_____
_____
_____
_____
_____
_____

Lessons / Modules that I have found to be particularly helpful or interesting:

_____
_____
_____
_____
_____

Course title: _____

Instructor name: _____

Date of purchase: _____ Amount Paid: _____

Email address used for purchase: _____

Date email confirmation was received: _____

Email confirmation sent from: _____

Order # from email confirmation: _____

Does course come with a satisfaction guarantee?   Yes / No   If yes,
when does guarantee expire? _____

Lifetime access to course material? Yes / No   If no, when does access
expire? _____

Log in URL: _____

User name: _____ Password: _____

Is any bonus content included with purchase?   Yes / No

If yes, list bonus content and when it is to be released here:

_____

_____

_____

_____

_____

_____

_____

_____

Lessons / Modules that I have found to be particularly helpful or interesting:

_____

_____

_____

_____

_____

Course title: _____

Instructor name: _____

Date of purchase: _____ Amount Paid: _____

Email address used for purchase: _____

Date email confirmation was received: _____

Email confirmation sent from: _____

Order # from email confirmation: _____

Does course come with a satisfaction guarantee?   Yes / No   If yes,

when does guarantee expire? _____

Lifetime access to course material?   Yes / No   If no, when does access

expire? _____

Log in URL: _____

User name: _____ Password: _____

Is any bonus content included with purchase?   Yes / No

If yes, list bonus content and when it is to be released here:

_____

_____

_____

_____

_____

_____

_____

_____

Lessons / Modules that I have found to be particularly helpful or interesting:

_____

_____

_____

_____

_____

Course title: _____

Instructor name: _____

Date of purchase: _____ Amount Paid: _____

Email address used for purchase: _____

Date email confirmation was received: _____

Email confirmation sent from: _____

Order # from email confirmation: _____

Does course come with a satisfaction guarantee?   Yes / No   If yes, when does guarantee expire? _____

Lifetime access to course material? Yes / No   If no, when does access expire? _____

Log in URL: _____

User name: _____ Password: _____

Is any bonus content included with purchase?   Yes / No

If yes, list bonus content and when it is to be released here:

_____

_____

_____

_____

_____

_____

_____

_____

Lessons / Modules that I have found to be particularly helpful or interesting:

_____

_____

_____

_____

_____

Course title: _____

Instructor name: _____

Date of purchase: _____ Amount Paid: _____

Email address used for purchase: _____

Date email confirmation was received: _____

Email confirmation sent from: _____

Order # from email confirmation: _____

Does course come with a satisfaction guarantee?   Yes / No   If yes,

when does guarantee expire? _____

Lifetime access to course material? Yes / No   If no, when does access

expire? _____

Log in URL: _____

User name: _____ Password: _____

Is any bonus content included with purchase?   Yes / No

If yes, list bonus content and when it is to be released here:

_____

_____

_____

_____

_____

_____

_____

_____

_____

Lessons / Modules that I have found to be particularly helpful or interesting:

_____

_____

_____

_____

_____

Course title: _____

Instructor name: _____

Date of purchase: _____ Amount Paid: _____

Email address used for purchase: _____

Date email confirmation was received: _____

Email confirmation sent from: _____

Order # from email confirmation: _____

Does course come with a satisfaction guarantee?   Yes / No   If yes,

when does guarantee expire? _____

Lifetime access to course material? Yes / No   If no, when does access

expire? _____

Log in URL: _____

User name: _____ Password: _____

Is any bonus content included with purchase?   Yes / No

If yes, list bonus content and when it is to be released here:

_____

_____

_____

_____

_____

_____

_____

_____

_____

Lessons / Modules that I have found to be particularly helpful or interesting:

_____

_____

_____

_____

_____

Course title: _____

Instructor name: _____

Date of purchase: _____ Amount Paid: _____

Email address used for purchase: _____

Date email confirmation was received: _____

Email confirmation sent from: _____

Order # from email confirmation: _____

Does course come with a satisfaction guarantee?   Yes / No   If yes,
when does guarantee expire? _____

Lifetime access to course material? Yes / No   If no, when does access
expire? _____

Log in URL: _____

User name: _____ Password: _____

Is any bonus content included with purchase?   Yes / No

If yes, list bonus content and when it is to be released here:

_____

_____

_____

_____

_____

_____

_____

_____

Lessons / Modules that I have found to be particularly helpful or interesting:

_____

_____

_____

_____

_____

Course title: _____

Instructor name: _____

Date of purchase: _____ Amount Paid: _____

Email address used for purchase: _____

Date email confirmation was received: _____

Email confirmation sent from: _____

Order # from email confirmation: _____

Does course come with a satisfaction guarantee?   Yes / No   If yes,
when does guarantee expire? _____

Lifetime access to course material? Yes / No   If no, when does access
expire?   _____

Log in URL: _____

User name: _____ Password: _____

Is any bonus content included with purchase?   Yes / No

If yes, list bonus content and when it is to be released here:

_____

_____

_____

_____

_____

_____

_____

_____

_____

Lessons / Modules that I have found to be particularly helpful or interesting:

_____

_____

_____

_____

_____

Course title: _____

Instructor name: _____

Date of purchase: _____ Amount Paid: _____

Email address used for purchase: _____

Date email confirmation was received: _____

Email confirmation sent from: _____

Order # from email confirmation: _____

Does course come with a satisfaction guarantee?   Yes / No   If yes,

when does guarantee expire? _____

Lifetime access to course material? Yes / No   If no, when does access

expire? _____

Log in URL: _____

User name: _____ Password: _____

Is any bonus content included with purchase?   Yes / No

If yes, list bonus content and when it is to be released here:

_____

_____

_____

_____

_____

_____

_____

_____

Lessons / Modules that I have found to be particularly helpful or interesting:

_____

_____

_____

_____

_____

Course title: _____

Instructor name: _____

Date of purchase: _____ Amount Paid: _____

Email address used for purchase: _____

Date email confirmation was received: _____

Email confirmation sent from: _____

Order # from email confirmation: _____

Does course come with a satisfaction guarantee?   Yes / No   If yes, when does guarantee expire? _____

Lifetime access to course material? Yes / No   If no, when does access expire? _____

Log in URL: _____

User name: _____ Password: _____

Is any bonus content included with purchase?   Yes / No

If yes, list bonus content and when it is to be released here:

_____

_____

_____

_____

_____

_____

_____

_____

Lessons / Modules that I have found to be particularly helpful or interesting:

_____

_____

_____

_____

_____

Course title: _____

Instructor name: _____

Date of purchase: _____ Amount Paid: _____

Email address used for purchase: _____

Date email confirmation was received: _____

Email confirmation sent from: _____

Order # from email confirmation: _____

Does course come with a satisfaction guarantee?   Yes / No   If yes,

When does guarantee expire? _____

Lifetime access to course material? Yes / No   If no, when does access

expire? _____

Log in URL: _____

User name: _____ Password: _____

Any bonus content included with purchase?   Yes / No

If yes, list bonus content and when it is to be released here:

_____
_____
_____
_____
_____
_____
_____
_____

Lessons / Modules that I have found to be particularly helpful or interesting:

_____
_____
_____
_____
_____

Course title: _____

Instructor name: _____

Date of purchase: _____ Amount Paid: _____

Email address used for purchase: _____

Date email confirmation was received: _____

Email confirmation sent from: _____

Order # from email confirmation: _____

Does course come with a satisfaction guarantee?   Yes / No   If yes,
when does guarantee expire? _____

Lifetime access to course material?   Yes / No   If no, when does access
expire? _____

Log in URL: _____

User name: _____ Password: _____

Is any bonus content included with purchase?   Yes / No

If yes, list bonus content and when it is to be released here:

_____

_____

_____

_____

_____

_____

_____

_____

Lessons / Modules that I have found to be particularly helpful or interesting:

_____

_____

_____

_____

_____

Made in the USA
San Bernardino, CA
09 November 2019

59694766R00058